The Greatest Enemies
of the Church

in the 21st Century

The Greatest Enemies of the Church

in the 21st Century

by

Matt Costella

Fundamental Evangelistic Association
Fresno, California

The Greatest Enemies of the Church in the 21st Century

Copyright © 2012
Fundamental Evangelistic Association

All rights reserved. No part of this book may be reproduced in any form, except for the inclusion of brief quotations in a review or article, without written permission from the author or publisher.

All Scripture quotations are taken from the
King James Version of the Bible

To order additional copies of this book or to inquire about pricing information, please contact:

Fundamental Evangelistic Association
2251 E. Beechwood Ave.
Fresno, California 93720
(559) 298-4574 (phone)
www.feasite.org

ISBN: 978-0-9718516-1-0

Printed in the United States by Morris Publishing®
3212 East Highway 30
Kearney, NE 68847
1-800-650-7888

Dedicated to my father,

Dennis Costella,

who was known for his love for the Truth and his desire to always be of help and encouragement to others.

Table of Contents

Introduction — page 8

Enemy #1: False Doctrine — page 11

Enemy #2: Emotionalism — page 23

Enemy #3: Pragmatism — page 31

Enemy #4: Worldliness — page 41

Enemy #5: Apathy/Indifference — page 55

Enemy #6: Distraction/Diversion — page 65

Introduction

Since its inception, the church of Jesus Christ has endured one attack after another from the "god of this world" who is intent on destroying God's children by any means possible. Even today, 2000 years after the birth of the church, God's people are being relentlessly battered by ideas and philosophies that often *sound* tenable yet are, in reality, completely opposed to the will and Word of God. Of course, God knew this would happen. He told us that in the age in which we live, people (including professing believers) would "not endure sound doctrine" but would, instead, "turn away their ears from the truth" as they listened only to those religious leaders who would tell them what they wanted to hear (2 Tim. 4:3-4).

Every honest Christian will admit that the church is under attack in some form and that enemies of the church exist with the intent of undermining the truth and rendering believers ineffective as ministers of Jesus Christ. Yet almost every Christian will have his or her own list of what he or she believes constitutes the "greatest enemies of the church" today. However, such a "list" oftentimes portrays only the *symptoms* of a sick church rather than the *root* problems. The purpose of this book is to dig down deeper—to realize that the many problems that exist today stem from attitudes, philosophies, and beliefs that produce shallow churches and sick Christians. These inward problems and issues are the foundation of one's outward actions and behavior. Jesus made it clear in Matthew 15:18 that "those things which proceed out of the mouth come forth from the heart; and they defile the man." Clearly, one must fight these enemies by first realizing their root source—the heart of man. Of course, *people* comprise the church. Therefore, the enemies that plague the church begin with the beliefs, behavior, and attitudes of individual *people*.

The "list" of enemies given in this book is by no means exhaustive. At the same time, I believe this list is highly accurate, and the enemies described herein are real and dangerous. God has revealed that Satan does not possess any secret weapons. In fact, the darts he hurls toward the church today are the same darts he has hurled toward God's people for thousands of years. The apostle Paul wrote that "we are not ignorant of [Satan's] devices" (2 Cor. 2:11), and he assured us that Satan cannot come up with any new weapon that he has not used before (1 Cor. 10:13a).

Despite the fact that the church is being attacked and powerful enemies exist, God has given His church clear instruction concerning how to do battle against this constant onslaught. And not only that, He has given us one example after another in His Word of those who have faced the same foes—the same enemies—we face today. This book encourages God's people to recognize these enemies and to consider those individuals recorded in Scripture who have gone on before us and serve as good examples and bad examples concerning how to wage these daily battles. We must allow God's Word to teach us through precept and example. We must study the Scriptures with a receptive heart and a willingness to be challenged and changed. Only then will we be able to be victorious against our foe.

Be encouraged in the Lord. Be aware of your enemies. Be resolute and determined to follow Jesus Christ and remain faithful to Him at all cost. It may be difficult now, but rest and reward await those who love and obey the Savior.

Enemy #1: False Doctrine

The Reality of False Doctrine

Ask Christians in any church if they believe false doctrine exists, and they will likely admit that something called "false doctrine" or "false teaching" truly exists. Yet, ask the same Christians in the same church if they or their church embraces or propagates false doctrine, and their answer will most likely be something like this: "Not my church"; or maybe, "Not that I am aware of"; or even, "I don't think so." You see, false teaching is something that always finds a home "out there" in some other person, church, denomination, or sect. But is it possible that even good churches and sincere Christians can be guilty of believing or teaching false doctrine?

False teaching, or false doctrine, is simply any teaching propagated or embraced that conflicts with the truth as revealed in the Word of God. Most people who embrace false doctrine actually point to Scripture to support their errant beliefs. Yes, people can make the Bible say anything they want it to say. This is why it is so important to grasp the *context* of every passage of Scripture.

The goal of the faithful Christian is to understand God's Word as God meant it to be understood to the reader. Remember, even Satan himself used the Bible to "proof text" his claims as he tempted Jesus in the wilderness. Yet Jesus replied with Scripture *accurately interpreted!*

The word *doctrine* simply means "teaching." Yes, false doctrine does exist. In fact, it has existed since the beginning of time. Thousands of years ago in the garden of Eden, the serpent propagated the first "false doctrine" recorded in the history of mankind when he told Eve, "Ye shall not surely die" (Gen. 3:4). God had declared to Adam and Eve that they could eat of any fruit of the trees of the garden except the Tree of the Knowledge of Good and Evil. God told them that should they eat of this tree, they would certainly die. The serpent declared otherwise. God declared the truth, and the serpent contradicted it with false doctrine, or erroneous teaching.

Since this first incident in the garden of Eden, Satan has continued to propagate false teaching, for "he is a liar, and the father of it" (Jn. 8:44). Christians who comprise the church, the body of Christ in this age, are not without warning concerning the reality and abundance of false teaching. The New Testament Scriptures warn the believer that false teaching—even within the professing church—will be a hallmark characteristic of the church age, the age of grace.

Jesus Himself hated false teaching and decried the religious leaders of His day for misleading the Jews through their words and their walk. Notice Matthew 16:6-12. Here, Jesus warned His disciples of the "leaven" or "doctrine" (v. 12) of the Pharisees and Sadducees. In the context, these religious leaders were looking for a "sign" from Jesus rather than receiving Him as their Messiah and changing their hearts. Jesus called them "blind guides" (Matt. 23:16, 24) and "hypocrites" who were void of discernment (Matt. 16:3), and yet these men were revered as the leading rabbis of the day who were responsible to impart spiritual knowledge to the children of Israel.

Following the death and resurrection of Jesus and the birth of the church, false doctrine continued to find its home in the hearts and minds of many within and without the church. The apostle Paul told the elders in Ephesus to "take heed" to themselves and to God's "flock" because after Paul left them, false teachers—including some of the church elders—would "arise, speaking perverse things, to draw away disciples" (Acts 20:29-30). Even in the church at Ephesus, false teaching was a serious problem!

Interestingly enough, many of the New Testament epistles (letters) were written to address false teaching that had crept into the church. Paul, Peter, John, Jude, and others penned Holy Spirit-inspired letters to individuals and churches for the purpose of setting the record straight—declaring the truth over against doctrinal error. Consider several letters (books of the New Testament) written for the purpose of addressing false doctrine:

1. *Galatians*—written to address the problem of legalism proclaimed by the Judaizers.

2. *Colossians*—written to address the problem of Gnosticism making its way into the church.

3. *2 Thessalonians*—written to address the problem of false teaching concerning the rapture and the tribulation.

4. *Hebrews*—written to Christians who were backsliding into spiritual lethargy and leaning toward Judaistic legalism.

5. *1 John* and *2 John*—written to Christians who were facing the Gnostic heresies that diminished the person of Jesus Christ (1 Jn. 2:26; 4:1-6; 2 Jn. 7-11).

6. *Revelation*—Chapters two and three were written to local churches in Asia Minor, some of which were embracing error or minimizing the dangers of false doctrine.

Yet what is especially notable about God's Word is that it not only addresses those in the first century but it also addresses believers in the twenty-first century as well! Carefully read and consider the following New Testament texts, which clearly reveal that false teaching exists and even abounds as the end of the church age draws near:

1 Timothy 4:1—The Holy Spirit clearly declares that as the end of the age draws near, people will turn from the truth as they give their attention to teaching that is demon-inspired rather than Holy Spirit-inspired. This text is quite informative, for it reveals that the catalyst of their departure from "the faith" was their attention to false doctrine.

2 Timothy 4:1-4—Paul tells Timothy (and all believers today) that people will come to a point where they no longer endure the truth but, rather, will turn away from the truth and listen to myths (un-truths). The truth is not popular with the world because it is exclusive and narrow. Because of this, many did not endure it and chose a broad and easy path, and "fables" or false teaching filled the void left by truth.

2 Peter 2:1-2—Peter reminds his readers that just as false prophets existed in the Old Testament times, false teachers will intermingle among believers even today, and these false teachers will introduce extremely dangerous teaching into the church. This text is interesting because it reveals that *many* will follow the false teachers, and it informs us that this false teaching will be introduced to the church subtly and craftily. In other words, undiscerning people would not even recognize the false teaching when it crept into the church.

2 Peter 3:1-3, 17—Peter reminds believers in the church that scoffers will arise who will mock and deny the clear teaching of God's Word. Obviously, these men and women will have their own sets of beliefs that contradict the truth, and these errant beliefs will stem from their own "lusts" (v. 3), that is, they will believe and behave in a manner that suits their own desires.

Jude 1-25—The entire letter from Jude urges believers to beware of the false teaching of those who are attempting to seduce them away from the truth. These false teachers are wicked and arrogant, yet they appear pleasant and cordial on the outside. They tell people what they want to hear, even though their words are empty of truth and dangerous to the spiritual lives of God's people. Yes, sound doctrine is of paramount importance to God. The Bible itself is full of truth and full of warnings concerning error. Never let anyone declare that doctrine is not important. It is of paramount importance to the church today. Dr. Renald Showers in his book *The Foundations of Faith* wrote the following words:

> Is it true that doctrine is not important? God doesn't think so. Many years ago I read an article that so impressed me I have never forgotten its content. At the beginning of a seminary course on New Testament studies, an instructor told his students that they would work together on one major project that semester. They would move systematically through the New Testament to categorize every area of truth and determine how many times each area is addressed. Their goal was to find the one truth emphasized more than any other in the New Testament. When they completed the project, they were amazed to see that warning against false doctrine is emphasized more than any other issue—even more than love, unity, and experience.
>
> Since God inspired the Scriptures, this discovery is significant. It indicates that doctrine is of paramount importance to God. Since it is so important to Him, it had better be important to His people (p. 10).

The Ramifications of False Doctrine

Although the ramifications of false doctrine in the life of a believer and the church are many, take some time to consider four primary consequences of such:

1. It leads to ungodly behavior.

What one *believes* determines how he *behaves*. To pay attention to false teaching only leads to more ungodliness (2 Tim. 2:16). Notice that in 1 Timothy 4:1-3, those who are embracing and teaching false doctrine are behaving in a manner that is completely inconsistent with truth. The believer cannot divorce his beliefs from his behavior. God's Word is full of examples of people who dishonored the Lord with their behavior because inwardly they lacked belief in His promises and commands.

2. It can lead to more doctrinal error and eventually shipwreck the faith of a believer.

Erroneous beliefs can lead to doubt and despair (2 Tim. 2:16-18). This can often affect believers to the degree that they move away from faith and confidence in God and His Word and "fall from [their] own stedfastness" (2 Pet. 3:17; 1 Tim. 1:19). Second Timothy 4:3-4 says that those who turn away their ears from the truth turn their ears toward something else—fables or myths (that which is not literally true). This, of course, only leads to a spiritual disaster. In 1 Corinthians 15:12, Paul declared the truth of future resurrection and spelled out the dangerous implications of rejecting this doctrine (that is, if resurrection is not a reality, then Jesus did not rise again, the Christian's faith is vain, he has no hope, etc.). False teaching in its many forms does not edify (build up) Christians. On the contrary, it tears them down and brings despair and even spiritual ruin.

3. It will destroy the unity of the church.

The common ground of believers is described in Scripture as "the faith," that is, the body of truth that has been delivered to the church (Acts 16:5; 1 Cor. 16:13; Eph. 4:5; Col. 2:7; 2 Tim. 4:7; Jude 3). The apostle Paul frequently exhorted the New Testament churches to be unified in "the faith," and this is accomplished through a unity of mind and purpose (Rom. 15:5-6; Phil. 1:27). In fact, God has gifted His church with pastor-teachers to equip saints to do the work of the ministry as they hold fast sound doctrine and are mature enough to withstand being tossed about with every wind of doctrine. Ephesians 4:11-16 addresses the importance of doctrine, unity, spiritual maturity, and the dangers of false teaching in the church. False doctrine destroys the unity that God desires of His body.

4. It will render a believer unusable for God.

Clearly, to depart from "the faith" or to teach that which is contrary to the truth renders one ineffective in ministry. In 2 Timothy 3:13-17, the apostle Paul makes it clear that Timothy was to "continue" in the truth he had learned, understanding that the Holy Scriptures were totally sufficient to bring him to spiritual maturity. In verse seventeen, it is evident that only the one who continues in truth (as opposed to error or false teaching) is mature and equipped to do what is right for God's glory. The Christian who is usable for God is one who is separated from iniquity (including bad doctrine) and set apart unto the Lord, "prepared unto every good work" (2 Tim. 2:19, 21). God wants to use every believer for His glory, but the Christian is only "usable" when he is separated from sin and set apart unto God.

The Remedy for False Doctrine

Although false doctrine has been around since the beginning of time, and although God reminds His children in His Word that they will continue to face this formidable foe until the end of the age, He has given clear instructions concerning how to avoid the snare of this great enemy of the church. Consider five necessary action steps:

1. Be aware and reminded of its continual presence within and without the church.

Awareness is the first line of defense. Too often, Christians today live life with their heads in the clouds, not even *remembering* that a real enemy exists and is trying to destroy the church through false doctrine. God knows that believers tend to be forgetful and susceptible to this dangerous enemy, so He constantly exhorts the church to "remember." Jude writes, "But, beloved, remember ye the words which were spoken before of the apostles of our Lord Jesus Christ; How that they told you there should be mockers in the last time ..." (Jude 17-18). The apostle Peter told the Christians in the early church that they needed to be continually reminded of the truths of God's Word (2 Pet. 1:12-15). In fact, he noted that the words he wrote (inspired by the Holy Spirit) would serve as a continual reminder even after he died and went to be with the Lord (2 Pet. 1:15). Notice what he said concerning his authorship of the second epistle: "This second epistle, beloved, I now write unto you; in both which I stir up your pure minds by way of remembrance: That ye may be mindful of the words which were spoken before. ... Knowing this first, that there shall come in the last days scoffers, walking after their own lusts" (2 Pet. 3:1-3). Do not forget that false doctrine not only exists in the church, but it will increase as time goes on!

2. Be grounded and established in the truth.

Of course, the best *defense* is a good *offense*. God's program for this age centers around the church, and the primary focus of the church is to propagate the truth. Believers must be rooted and grounded and steadfast in *the faith* (Col. 2:6-7). Without a good grounding in the truth, it is impossible to be protected from false doctrine. Consider the following texts and notice the common thread that runs through each of them:

Second Timothy 2:15 exhorts every Christian to "study" as a "workman" who is "rightly dividing the word of truth." The word *study* carries the idea of diligent persistence in working hard to effectively ground oneself in properly interpreting and applying the truth to one's life and ministry.

Second Timothy 3:14-17 reveals that the Old and New Testament Scriptures are totally sufficient to equip the believer to be a mature Christian who manifests a close walk with God. The Holy Scriptures are not only able to save a sinner, but they are also able to "grow" or "mature" a saint. All Scripture is "profitable for doctrine, for reproof, for correction, for instruction in righteousness: That the man of God may be perfect (mature), throughly furnished unto all good works." Believers need to be grounded in God's Word in order to recognize false doctrine and to remove themselves from it.

Second Timothy 4:2 is God's call for a constant emphasis on His Word. Timothy is told to "preach the Word" without compromise, and he is to accomplish this goal as he exercises patience and longsuffering while paying attention to "doctrine."

Second Peter 3:17-18 is an excellent summary of the apostle Peter's letter, for it not only encourages believers to be reminded of the truth and to beware of error, but it describes how they can keep from falling from their own "stedfastness"—by growing in "grace, and in the knowledge of our Lord and Saviour Jesus Christ." Followers of Jesus Christ need to be established and steadfast in the truth of God's Word (healthy, true doctrine) in order to battle the onslaught of error.

3. Judge (examine) yourself.

Believers must not think that they can live their lives on "autopilot." If a Christian is growing spiritually, he will be constantly changing and conforming to the image of Jesus Christ. During his spiritual growth process, he will be confronted with false teaching and false teachers at times. This is simply a part of life. Satan, who is described as the "god of this world," will continually find ways to introduce God's people to thoughts, beliefs, and worldviews that contradict the truth as revealed in the person of Jesus Christ and His Word, the Bible. Therefore, believers must keep checking up on themselves! The apostle John reminds the church that "many deceivers are entered into the world" and then exhorts Christians to "look to yourselves, that we lose not those things which we have wrought, but that we receive a full reward" (2 Jn. 7-8). Believers must not be self-deceived and think they are exempt from falling prey to Satan's devices.

4. Avoid that which is false.

People today do not like to be told to *avoid* or *separate* from anything. Yet avoidance of error is the only way to be spiritually healthy. Just as in the physical realm one must avoid junk food if he wants to be physically healthy, in the spiritual realm he must avoid "junk doctrine" if he wants to be spiritually healthy. Consider God's clear commands to separate from (avoid) false doctrine:

Romans 16:17 is one of the clearest passages of Scripture on the subject of separation from false doctrine and those who embrace it. Paul tells the Roman Christians, "Mark them which cause divisions and offences contrary to the doctrine which ye have learned; and avoid them." Notice that *doctrine*—not personalities or opinions or any other issue—is the dividing line here. Paul was concerned that false teachers would arise and "deceive the hearts of the simple" through their "good words and fair speeches" (Rom. 16:18). Remember, false doctrine does not look "evil." Rather, it appeals not only to the one who propagates it but to the listener as well.

Second Timothy 2:16-19 exhorts believers to "shun (keep away from; avoid) profane and vain babblings" and to "depart from iniquity." Notice that the context of these iniquitous teachings centered around a denial of the truth (the doctrine of the resurrection) and a propagation of error. Paul knew that to embrace this teaching could have a profoundly negative impact on one's life.

Second Thessalonians 3:14-15 is a command to avoid or separate from a Christian brother who walks disorderly, yet notice that the "dividing line" between avoidance and acceptance is whether or not this individual obeys "our [the apostle's] word by this epistle." The teaching of the New Testament apostles and prophets as penned in Scripture is of paramount importance in the life of a follower of Jesus Christ, and those who ignore, reject, or disobey the truth are to be avoided, even if they are fellow brothers or sisters in Christ.

Please note, however, that one's "separatist" attitude is extremely important. Paul writes, "Yet count him not as an enemy, but admonish him as a brother."

5. Test all teachings according to the standard of God's Word, the Bible.

The Word of God is the only certain, objective standard of truth. To measure a teaching against another person or against the beliefs and values of a majority of people or against history or anything else is insufficient. People change. Ideas and philosophies change. But God and His Word are solid and unchangeable. Therefore, if a believer is to be rooted, grounded, and established in the truth, then he must measure every teaching and philosophy and behavior according to this objective standard of truth.

In 1 John 4:1-6, the apostle John warns Christians to "believe not every spirit ... because many false prophets are gone out into the world" (v. 1). It is evident from this text that dangerous doctrine is not only demon-inspired, but it comes in the form of *people* who are spreading this false doctrine. John's exhortation to the church is to "try the spirits whether they are of God" (v. 1). How can Christians do this? They can do so by measuring the words and actions of these teachers against the Scriptures. John writes, "He that knoweth God heareth us (the apostles and prophets); he that is not of God heareth not us. Hereby know we the spirit of truth, and the spirit of error" (v. 6). In other words, if any doctrine conflicts with the teachings of the authors of God's Word—the Bible—then such a doctrine is "false doctrine," and those who propagate it are dangerous and should be avoided.

Notice 2 Thessalonians 2:15. Here, Paul exhorts the believers in Thessalonica (and all Christians today) to "stand fast, and hold the traditions which ye have been taught, whether by word, or our epistle." Again, it is evident that the dividing line between what one should embrace or reject is the doctrine proclaimed by the authors of Scripture. In 2 Thessalonians 3:4-6 the apostle Paul again commands the saints in Thessalonica to use God's authoritative Word ("the tradition which he received of us") as the ultimate standard by which all belief and behavior are to be judged.

Conclusion

That false doctrine is all around us is a daunting reality. Yet God has given His children the keys to spiritual victory. First, they possess the truth (Jn. 17:17). Nothing is more liberating, eternal, and powerful than the truth as it is in the person of God and the Word of God. Second, they have been blessed with the power of God through the indwelling ministry of the Holy Spirit. With God's Word and the indwelling Holy Spirit, a believer can have victory over any foe. "Now unto Him that is able to keep you from falling, and to present you faultless before the presence of His glory with exceeding joy, To the only wise God our Saviour, be glory and majesty, dominion and power, both now and ever. Amen" (Jude 24-25).

Enemy #2: Emotionalism

What Is Emotionalism?

In a strictly secular sense, emotionalism entails the formulation of policies or decisions based solely upon subjective feelings (emotions) rather than objective truth. So in its simplest form, emotionalism means to base one's choices upon how one feels. In a spiritual or theological sense, however, the concept of emotionalism entails basing one's spiritual decisions and priorities upon emotion and feeling; it is to be led or controlled by emotion (how one feels) rather than fact or knowledge (what one thinks or knows to be true).

The Problem of Emotionalism

Many Christians today are making spiritual decisions based upon how they *feel* rather than what they *know* to be true. This is true in the grand scheme of things (like what church one should attend or who a person should marry) as well as in the daily routine of life (like whether or not one should attend church on a particular day or whether or not one should take time to study God's Word and pray). People have a natural tendency to look for excitement or drama. They want to *feel* something. Yet when it comes to the spiritual lives and priorities of those who know Jesus Christ as Savior, emotionalism is an extremely dangerous enemy of the church for several reasons.

1. Emotions cannot be trusted.

We need to understand that the way we *do* feel does not always translate into the way we *should* feel. As sinful human beings, we have a natural tendency to succumb to worry, even though God tells us that He is in control; to lust, even though God tells us that to do so can be sin; to despair, even though our focus on God should bring joy; to hate (or be angry), even though to do so is toxic in our relationships (Col. 3:8); to envy (or be jealous) even though God declares such to be idolatry (Col. 3:5). The point is this—we cannot trust our emotions because they can and will betray us at times. Even though we may *feel* worried, hateful, angry, envious, etc., such emotions are clearly contrary to God's will for those who have a personal relationship with Him.

2. Emotions are relative to each person.

While truth is objective, feelings are subjective. One person might want to feel "high" while another person might enjoy feeling "low." These feelings can impact the choices and behavior one displays in the spiritual realm. For example, the person who wants a "high" might look for a church that gives an upbeat feeling while the person who wants a "low" might look for a church that is contemplative and quiet. So the right "fit" in this instance is not determined by *truth* (the church's doctrinal stance or philosophy of ministry) but by the individual and his or her *feelings* and emotional desires. If God allowed Christians to seek truth or morality through the way they felt at a particular point in time, Christianity would be a mass confusion of meaningless mush! Sadly, much of professing Christendom today seems to be this very thing because people are guilty of living according to their feelings rather than God's objective truth.

3. Emotions can actually lead one to do the opposite of God's will.

Making spiritual decisions and organizing life's priorities according to feelings and emotions can actually result in a believer doing the *opposite* of what God desires. The Bible is full of historical examples of men and women who knew what God had declared (objective truth), yet they chose to behave according to their feelings and subsequently reaped devastating consequences. Consider several such examples:

Eve and the forbidden fruit (Gen. 3:6)—Eve knew what God had commanded. In fact, she repeated to the serpent God's clear command (Gen. 3:2-3). Yet she wanted the "high" of the aesthetic enjoyment of the fruit (look and taste) as well as the feeling of power (knowledge). Her emotions led her to disobey God.

Cain and Abel (Gen. 4:5-6)—Cain was full of anger and hatred toward Abel even though he knew exactly what was right and pleasing to God (Gen. 4:7). His emotions caused him to kill his own brother.

Joseph's brothers (Gen. 37:4, 11, 20)—These men had feelings of hatred and jealousy toward Joseph because their father favored him above themselves. These feelings led them to talk of killing their brother. Eventually, they sold Joseph into slavery instead, although doing so was a grave offense against their father and against God.

Moses and the rock in the wilderness (Num. 20:1-12)—In the wilderness, the people murmured and complained against God and against Moses and Aaron. Moses became extremely angry toward the people and their ungrateful attitude. Rather than obeying God's command and speaking to the rock, Moses' feelings of anger and frustration led him to demonstrate a lack of obedience and faith. He struck the rock even though doing so defied God's clear Word.

Elijah under attack (1 Kgs. 19:1-4, 9-10)—Elijah felt lonely and depressed as Jezebel sought his life; he felt as though he was the only prophet of God left in the land. He despaired even of life itself. And yet notice God's response: "What are you doing here?" (vv. 9, 13); "Get back to work doing what I have called you to do" (vv. 15-17); "You are not alone" (v. 18). Elijah's emotions led him to despair and inactivity even though God had clearly called him to continue pressing forward in ministry.

Solomon's quest for happiness, wisdom, and life's meaning (Eccl. 1:16-2:17)—The wisest man who ever lived sought every positive emotion possible in an effort to bring joy and satisfaction to his life. He describes his quest and his feelings in Ecclesiastes chapters one and two. Yet Solomon discovered that apart from the fear and knowledge of God, "all was vanity and vexation of spirit" (Eccl. 2:11).

Jeremiah and his depression (Jer. 20:7-9)—The message Jeremiah proclaimed to God's people was not well-received, even to the point that Jeremiah did not feel like proclaiming it anymore at all! He wanted to quit. He felt as though God had given him a burden that he could not bear. Yet, God had made it extremely clear when he called Jeremiah that He would be with him no matter what he experienced (Jer. 1:4-9).

Jonah and the Assyrians (Jonah 4:1-3)—Jonah's hatred of the Assyrians and his negative feelings toward God's mercy caused him to clearly disobey God's call. Notice that ultimately it was Jonah's *feelings* toward the Assyrians (as well as his faith in God) that led to the whole mess in which he found himself. Had he simply obeyed God's command and refused to follow his feelings, he would not have had to face God's chastisement.

Peter and his mouth (Matt. 16:21-23; Jn. 18:25-27)—Sometimes it was his feelings of affection for Jesus (Matthew 16 text) and sometimes it was his feelings of fear for his life (John 18 text) that led Peter to say things that were in direct contradiction to truth. Yet regardless of the emotion (love or fear), Peter got himself into trouble when he acted on emotion rather than truth.

4. Emotions, therefore, can actually harm a believer's spiritual growth.

It is obvious from the many examples in Scripture that feelings are not an adequate guide or basis for decision-making in the Christian life. Ultimately, the problem is this: If a believer is looking for a "feeling" or if he or she is taking action or making personal choices based upon a "feeling," then he or she cannot be certain that the end product will be good or glorifying to God. In fact, it is clear from Scripture that following one's emotions rather than objective truth as revealed in Scripture can lead a believer *away* from proper fellowship with God and usefulness to Him.

So many people today are looking for a feeling when choosing a church; so many people today are resting upon a feeling when deciding on a spouse; so many people today are relying upon their emotions when choosing whether or not to take a stand for righteousness and truth in the home or workplace; so many people today are taking actions (or refusing to act) based upon their "feelings" or emotions rather than upon the objective truth of God as revealed to us in His Word. This should not—it *cannot*—be an option in the life of the faithful, God-honoring Christian.

Biblical Response to Emotionalism

1. Realize that emotions are not inherently evil.

God is a Person with emotion, and He created us in His image. Emotion in itself is not bad or wrong. God demonstrates grief (Gen. 6:6; Jn. 11:35, 38), anger (Num. 12:9), joy or pleasure (1 Kgs. 3:10), and other emotions. Almost all emotions, including anger, have their place in the plan and timing of God (Eccl. 3:4, 8). It is interesting to note that the only perfect Person to have ever lived—Jesus Christ—has given us a record of a portion of His life, and within that record one can find many different emotions. At times during His earthly life and ministry, Jesus demonstrated sadness, anger, joy, and other feelings. Christians must not fall into the trap of believing that emotion is, of itself, something evil to be eradicated from the life.

2. Understand that emotions have been affected by the fall.

Men and women—Christians included—cannot trust their emotions because sin has entered the picture of human existence. While feelings and emotions are not inherently evil, Christians must realize that sin has perverted every aspect of man's nature. Scripture reveals, time and again, that believers throughout history have ensnared themselves by following and trusting their emotions when such emotions conflicted with truth. So a simple awareness of sin's effect on man's feelings and emotions can go a long way in battling this enemy.

The apostle Paul declared with anguish, "For that which I do I allow not: for what I would, that do I not; but what I hate, that do I.... Now then it is no more I that do it, but sin that dwelleth in me. For I know that in me (that is, in my flesh,) dwelleth no good thing: for to will is present with me; but how to perform that which is good I find not. For the good that I would I do not: but the evil which I would not, that I do. Now if I do that I would not, it is no more I that do it, but sin that dwelleth in me" (Rom. 7:15-20). Yes, even the great apostle Paul struggled within himself. His emotions and desires were affected by the sin nature within Him.

3. Grasp the fact that a believer's basis for making choices must center on knowledge (truth) rather than emotion (feeling).

Every aspect of a Christian's spiritual life finds its rock-solid basis in knowledge, not emotion. This is true of salvation (1 Jn. 5:11-13) as well as the Christian life and spiritual walk following the new birth. Consider what the following texts teach concerning the basis of the Christian life:

1 Corinthians 15:58—Earlier in this chapter, the apostle Paul elaborates on the doctrine of the resurrection and the eventual glorified bodies of the saints. He noted that death has been conquered and God has given believers the victory through Jesus Christ (1 Cor. 15:57). Then, Paul uses the word *therefore* in verse 58 and exhorts believers to continue to abound in God's work because of the truths set forth in the previous verses. Christians are to be "stedfast, unmoveable, always abounding in the work of the Lord" whether they feel like it or not. The reality of a believer's victory through Christ and future resurrection hope is the basis for his persistence and diligence in ministry.

Ephesians 4:17-24—The entire thrust of this text is this: Christians must walk according to their new way of thinking and not according to the desires of the flesh—the way they walked prior to their salvation. A walk according to the "old man" (prior to one's salvation) is marked by selfishness, greed, sensuality, etc. (vv. 17-19). In other words, unbelievers live according to the desires of their flesh (how they feel). In contrast, those who know Jesus Christ are to walk according "as the truth is in Jesus" (v. 21) which entails "put[ting] on the new man" by being "renewed in the spirit of [their] mind" (vv. 23-24). Believers, unlike non-Christians, must walk according to truth rather than feeling or emotion.

Colossians 2:6-7—The believer's spiritual walk is to be rooted, grounded, and established upon the firm foundation of "the faith." Just as a Christian has received God's gift of eternal life by faith, he is to base his entire life—including all his choices and behavior—upon the revealed body of truth—God's Word—"the faith" (Jude 3).

1 Peter 1:18-2:2—The believer's redemption stems from the truth—the objective fact—of Jesus' substitutionary death and His resurrection, "that [our] faith and hope might be in God" (1:21).

Yet not only is his salvation rooted and based in factual truth, but now his obedience to the truth (1:22) leads him to continue to walk according to the truth rather than his feelings (2:1).

It is interesting to note that one could come up with many other texts exhorting the Christian to live a life of faithfulness to the truth, but no scriptural texts can be found to support one's need to follow his emotions when it comes to spirituality. Yet sadly, Christians today have found a way to do just that—they often blame their feelings and actions on the Holy Spirit. They will sometimes attribute their own feelings or actions to the Holy Spirit even though such feelings and actions contradict the truth of God's Word. Believers need to be very careful to avoid this at all cost!

Conclusion

The ultimate goal in the life of a child of God is to have emotion match truth. It is great to feel good, but make sure such feeling is wrapped up in the glory of God. It is fine to feel angry, but make sure that such feeling is also wrapped up in the glory of God. Ultimately, if one is in fellowship with Jesus Christ, he or she will be sensitive to the truth and express emotions in conjunction with the truth.

Enemy #3: Pragmatism

What Is Pragmatism?

The *Webster's College Dictionary* defines *pragmatism* as follows: "Character or conduct that emphasizes practical results or concerns rather than theory or principle; a philosophical movement or system having various forms, but generally stressing practical consequences as constituting the essential criterion in determining meaning, truth or value." In other words, *pragmatism* means "to take action based upon what seems to work." So, when using the term in the realm of Christianity or practical theology, the idea is this: We will discover what seems to work in order to meet our ministry goals, and we will then pursue our goals by utilizing the forms or systems that have produced the results we want.

In the secular realm, pragmatism has its proper place. For example, educators must find effective ways to stimulate the minds of students and hold their attention and then implement those methods in the classroom. Advertisers must discover what grabs and holds the attention of the consumer and then use those discoveries in promoting a particular product. Medical professionals must find the best method for treating a particular virus or disease and then inform their patients what they need to do in order to avoid or eradicate the ailment. Yet when it comes to one's spiritual walk, pragmatism is a serious danger and a real enemy in the church today.

Why Embrace Pragmatism in Ministry?

Some people embrace pragmatism in their Christian lives and ministries simply because it gets the results they want—they tend to believe that when it comes to spiritual goals, "the end justifies the means." This is the most obvious reason why many churches and ministries embrace a pragmatic philosophy of ministry. Many Christian books and seminars are geared toward showing people what they need to do in order to measure up to a certain standard or definition of success. Popular topics most often shrouded in a pragmatic philosophy of ministry include church growth and evangelism. People today want to know how the "big, successful" ministries became that way so they, too, can become big and successful in their own endeavors. They want to know how to "save more souls" and have a bigger impact on the world around them, and they believe that people who have demonstrated success in the eyes of men hold the answers.

Some embrace pragmatism because it is easier than the alternative. The fact of the matter is this: It is much easier to gain results than to be obedient and faithful to the clear commands of the Lord. Almost anybody can build a good-sized church or Christian ministry by simply doing what has worked for others. They can bring in the right band, hire the best motivational speakers or preachers, and implement programs that appeal to the spiritual seekers. Yet it is difficult to be big and successful in the eyes of men while simultaneously holding to a *biblical* model and philosophy of ministry.

It is important to realize that some embrace pragmatism because it is all they know or have known. Ignorance is the primary factor here. Some church leaders have been saved and discipled in churches and ministries steeped in pragmatic philosophy, and they simply do not see the dangers of pragmatism or even realize another alternative exists. In addressing the problem of pragmatism in the church, we must remember that God alone has the right to judge *the hearts* of those who practice this error, not us!

Biblical Examples of Pragmatism

God's Word is full of examples of men and women of faith who momentarily succumbed to this model of ministry. In every instance, God had given clear instruction and direction, yet His people chose to take a different path—a path that seemed to work from a human perspective but a path that proved to be disastrous in the end. Consider just a sampling of such incidents:

Saul sparing the life of Agag and cattle (1 Sam. 15:1-3, 7-23)— Saul claimed that he and the people were simply saving the best of the spoil to offer to the Lord for sacrifice. This excuse sounds extremely spiritual and pious. It seems as though God could not frown upon this. Yet God's command to Saul and the Israelites was clear: Destroy everything. God declared, "Now go and smite Amalek, and utterly destroy all that they have, and spare them not" (v. 3). God had made His will clearly known, yet Saul and the people of Israel had another plan that they felt "worked" better.

The "new cart" for the ark of the covenant (2 Sam. 6:1-11)— Of course, it was much easier to make a cart for the ark of the covenant and allow oxen to pull the ark rather than for the priests to have to carry it on their shoulders. Yet God had given explicit instructions for the transportation of the ark—the Levitical priests were to transport the ark on their shoulders (Deut. 10:8). Because God's holiness was violated and because His people disobeyed His instructions and chose to implement a "better" or "more effective" way to transport the ark, Uzzah lost his life. After this tragic event occurred, David learned his lesson and realized that the ark needed to be transported just as God had instructed (see 1 Chron.

15:1-3).

Solomon and his quest for happiness, wisdom, and meaning in life (Eccl. 1:16-2:11)—For a period of his life, Solomon purposed to discover what made him (and mankind in general) feel happiness and meaning in life. He did not withhold from himself anything that "appeared to work" from man's perspective when reaching for this goal. He turned to money, industry, music, sex, humor, and education in an effort to discover what would bring satisfaction and value to life. He wrote, "Whatsoever mine eyes desired I kept not from them, I withheld not my heart from any joy" (2:10). Yet all along, the fact of the matter was this: True joy and meaning in life can only be found in conjunction with the fear and knowledge of God, not with "trying out" all the world has to offer. Solomon finally concluded what he had known all along from the mouth of God: "Let us hear the conclusion of the whole matter: Fear God, and keep His commandments: for this is the whole duty of man" (12:13).

Jehoshaphat and Ahab's alliance (2 Chron. 18:1-34)—Jehoshaphat, king of Judah, allied himself with Ahab, one of the most wicked kings in Israel who continually defied the Lord. Maybe Jehoshaphat thought he could change Ahab through the marriage alliance between his son and Ahab's daughter (v. 1) or through his military alliance with this wicked king of Israel (vv. 2-3); or, maybe Jehoshaphat thought he could please God by claiming Ramothgilead for the Jews once again. Whatever his pragmatic intentions, Jehoshaphat thought it would "work" to enter into a compromised fellowship with a "disobedient brother," but God was greatly displeased by Jehoshaphat's compromise.

Gamaliel's advice to the religious leaders (Acts 5:33-42)—Gamaliel embraced a pragmatic approach to the truth. Rather than believing the words of the apostles—the truth given by God—Gamaliel chose to "wait and see" what would become of their teaching and their cause. He felt that the truthfulness of the message of the apostles would reveal itself in the *results* of the apostles' teachings. While it is true that "truth prevailed," Gamaliel's pragmatic approach to the truth is inconsistent with the will of God who desires that men repent and believe the gospel—not wait for a while to determine whether or not it has any merit in the eyes of men.

Not only does God's Word provide the reader with "good examples of bad examples"—people who succumbed to pragmatism—but it also describes those who did *not* give in to pragmatism even though doing so would have brought about better "results" from a human perspective.

Micaiah, the lone true prophet of God (2 Chron. 18:4-27)—Micaiah declared the true word of the Lord to Ahab when the king inquired (at the request of Jehoshaphat) whether or not he should go to battle. Even though all the false prophets of Ahab and Jezebel declared peace and safety to Ahab, Micaiah spoke the truth. He could have avoided prison had he gone along with all the other false prophets, but he remained true to God and faced the consequences.

Jeremiah and his unpopular message (Jer. 20:7-9)—The prophet Jeremiah obeyed the Lord and fulfilled what God had told him to do even though he was despised by his own people and few actually listened to him. As a result of obeying God, he was hated and ridiculed. He could have avoided a great amount of discomfort and scorn had he remained quiet, but he could not.

Paul and his method for evangelism and church planting (1 Thess. 2:1-6, 13)—The apostle Paul told the Thessalonian church that he had come to Thessalonica to declare the truth of the gospel without trickery or gimmicks. He likely could have gained a much wider audience—a greater following; far more "souls saved"—by using manipulative programs or catchy gimmicks to lure people into the church, but he refused to do so. Paul knew that God had simply called him to declare the truth, and the Holy Spirit would convict the hearts of men. Paul was not interested in numbers; he was interested in faithfulness to the Lord.

Peter and John threatened by the religious leaders (Acts 4:18-21)—When threatened and commanded by the religious leaders not to speak of Jesus anymore, Peter and John declared that they could not hold their peace concerning what they had seen and heard. They could have obeyed the religious leaders and remained quiet from that time forward, and everything would have "worked out" better for them from man's perspective. Yet they refused to take a pragmatic approach to ministry and, instead, continued to preach the gospel. For example, in Acts 5:27-29, the apostles were threatened *again* and accused of "fill[ing] Jerusalem with [their] doctrine." Yet they firmly declared that they would obey God rather than men, for God had clearly told them to proclaim the truth. Of course, they could have kept quiet or tried to formulate a "less offensive" message, but they realized that obedience to God is of paramount importance.

Problems with Pragmatism

Christians often embrace a pragmatic philosophy of ministry for a number of reasons, yet God's Word is full of timely examples of men and women who either succumbed to pragmatism and faced the consequences or who could have made their lives and ministries easier by embracing a pragmatic ministry outlook but chose, instead, to remain true to God's instructions for ministry. Two primary problems with a pragmatic philosophy and approach to ministry exist:

1. First, pragmatism stems from a faulty understanding of what constitutes "success."

Far too often, man's goals and definition of success are different—in fact, even contradictory—to what God has declared to be His desire for His people. Christians today often define success in terms of *numbers*—a successful church or ministry is one in which large numbers of people are present or involved or many people are being "saved" or making professions of faith; or in terms of *influence*—a successful person, church, or ministry is one marked by influence in the secular or religious community; or in terms of *approval* and *acceptance* by others—a successful ministry is well received by a majority of people.

But the fact of the matter is this: ***None*** of these things constitute biblical "success." Christians today can easily attempt to meet these "goals for success" through pragmatic means, yet this is not God's definition of success. In fact, to define success in terms of *numbers, influence,* or *acceptance* actually contradicts the truth as revealed by precept and example in the Scriptures.

2. Second, pragmatism ultimately results in disobedience and unfaithfulness to God.

The Bible makes it abundantly clear from Genesis to Revelation that *faithfulness*, not *success*, is God's requirement for Christian life and ministry. When a believer employs any form of pragmatism in his life and ministry (that is, he will do whatever seems to "work" from man's perspective in order to meet his spiritual goal), he will always find himself engaged in disobedience and unfaithfulness to the Lord. God declares that "My thoughts are not your thoughts, neither are your ways My ways, saith the LORD. For as the heavens are higher than the earth, so are My ways higher than your ways, and My thoughts than your thoughts" (Isa. 55:8-9). Man has his own concept of success—how to build a successful ministry, how to please God, how to reach out and help more people. Yet God's ways and thoughts are high above any ideas of men. It would behoove God's people to do ministry according to His ways as He has revealed them in His Word.

Biblical Response to Pragmatism

Both the Old Testament and New Testament Scriptures not only reveal God's displeasure with a pragmatic approach to ministry, but they also describe exactly what is God's will when it comes to living a life and engaging in a ministry that pleases and glorifies Him. Consider the following texts from both the Old and

New Testaments:

Micah 6:6-8—This is a key text that is applicable to the lives of all believers today. Far too often, Christians have a tendency to feel that as long as they are "doing enough" and "going through the motions" or having a "successful ministry" in the eyes of men, God will be pleased with their endeavors. Yet the Lord made it clear to His people that He wanted a relationship based upon righteousness, obedience, and truth. He was sick of all their empty sacrifices (vv. 6-7). From a human perspective, they seemed to be thriving spiritually as they offered abundant sacrifices to the Lord. Yet God knew their hearts, and He knew that their outward actions—while impressive in the eyes of men—were vain and empty because they were not faithful to Him in their hearts. What "worked" according to the flesh was an abomination to God.

1 Samuel 15:22-23—In this text, Samuel makes it clear to King Saul that obedience to the Word of God is what the Lord truly desires. God is not looking for believers to use all their human ingenuity and wisdom to impress Him. This is what King Saul and the people of Israel had tried to do—they disobeyed the Lord and then claimed that their actions were intended to honor God and to impress Him. Yet, "to obey is better than sacrifice, and to hearken than the fat of rams" (v. 22). God simply wants His people to be obedient and faithful to Him. The only way to be successful and meet spiritual goals that bring glory to God is to listen to His Word and then obey it!

Colossians 2:6-8—In this text, the apostle Paul makes it clear that a believer's Christian walk is not to be marked by pragmatism or ingenuity but by the very same characteristic that brought salvation in the first place—*faith*. God's command to His people is simple: Be established in *the faith* and continue to walk by faith through the knowledge of God's Word and obedience to it. *Faith* is the key here. In fact, Paul warns believers to "beware" of falling into the trap of thinking according to the mindset of the world (this can certainly include pragmatism in the Christian life and ministry) rather than embracing the mind of Christ (v. 8).

1 Thessalonians 2:1-6, 13—Paul tells the Thessalonian believers that when he arrived in Thessalonica to share the gospel and plant a church, he did not approach them using "pragmatic means." He did not use deceit or gimmicks or anything else to gain their trust. He simply sought to please God and declared the truth to them although he certainly could have acquired a larger following and a greater influence had he used pragmatic means to "win them to Christ."

1 Timothy 4:6, 15-16—Notice here that Paul exhorts Timothy—and all believers today—to "continue in" the truth of God's Word and be put in "remembrance" of *these* things (the healthy doctrine of Scripture) in order to be counted as good ministers of Jesus Christ. A truly faithful Christian will not seek out the latest spiritual trend, gimmick, or fad in an effort to build a bigger ministry or reach more people or exert more influence in the church and the world. The key here is to remember what God has said in His Word and *continue* in *these things*.

2 Timothy 3:14-17—Once again, the key to a "successful" Christian life and ministry from God's perspective is to "continue in" (v. 14) that which God has already established and declared to be true, that is, His Word. This is how every believer must define a truly successful ministry. He must measure his beliefs and behavior against "all Scripture," which is "profitable for doctrine, for reproof, for correction, for instruction in righteousness" (v. 16) as he strives to be "perfect" (spiritually mature) and demonstrates "good works" in life (v. 17). How is all this accomplished? Through continuing in the truth of God's Word.

2 Timothy 4:2-5—In this particular text, Paul warns believers that as time progresses, professing Christians in the church will not tolerate the truth. They will "not endure sound doctrine" (v. 3). In fact, they will surround themselves with pastors and teachers who tell them exactly what they want to hear. They will "turn away their ears from the truth, and shall be turned unto fables" (v. 4). Such a prognosis of the church is certainly dismal. Yet what is to be the response of the faithful minister of Christ? His response is not to find what "works" in order to get the attention of the masses who will not tolerate the truth; rather, the response of the faithful minister of Christ is to *keep preaching and teaching the Word* (vv. 2, 5)! God does not call believers to find new and ingenious ways to get people to pay attention, go to church, or change their lives. Rather, He wants His Word to be faithfully preached and taught even though many *will* refuse to listen.

Conclusion

It is interesting to note that in the New Testament, the apostle Paul told the elders of the church at Ephesus that he had faithfully fulfilled God's will as he declared the truth without compromise (Acts 20:17-32). He reminded them that he kept nothing back but had declared "all the counsel of God" (v. 27). However, this did not seem to "work" or be "successful" from man's viewpoint because false teaching and false teachers would eventually arise within the church at Ephesus (vv. 29-30). Yet despite the lack of "success," Paul remained faithful to what God had called him to do. Faithfulness and obedience, not "success," is God's requirement of His children.

Enemy #4: Worldliness

Contemporary Concepts of Worldliness

What exactly *is* worldliness? Many Christians are not aware that the Bible never uses the term *worldliness*. In fact, it only uses the term *worldly* twice—in Titus 2:12 and Hebrews 9:1—and only in the Titus passage does it address this concept of worldliness as it is used in the church today.

While worldliness is one of the greatest enemies of the church in the twenty-first century, it is imperative that believers truly understand what worldliness *is* and is *not*. Sadly, the concept of worldliness has been completely misunderstood in the modern church. Believers today must realize—or admit—that their idea of worldliness is often a totally unbiblical notion. One cannot grasp a *biblical* understanding of the concept of worldliness without starting anew and discarding the general (and usually flawed) ideas concerning what actually constitutes worldliness.

Today, when believers talk about worldliness, they often refer to certain *activities* that they deem to be "worldly." A discussion about worldliness often centers around what one wears, what one watches, what one listens to, and where one goes. For example, many believers think that to be "worldly" is to like or listen to a song or genre of music that is not generally accepted by the church or to like or watch a television show or movie (or even to attend a theater or have a television in your home). In other words, worldliness is synonymous with *activities* or things a person *does*. Many Christians are taught that if a believer keeps himself or herself from *doing* certain things, he or she is not guilty of the sin of worldliness. Yet in reality, this concept of worldliness has no biblical basis.

Often the church sets forth a list of definitions and parameters for worldliness—a list that it cannot actually defend from an honest interpretation of Scripture. Therefore, the church is facing devastating and heartbreaking consequences—young people are rebelling or leaving the church; divisions exist within churches between people who disagree on what does or does not constitute worldliness; people are losing interest in trying to live biblically because they discover that they cannot defend their beliefs and behavior with Scripture. It is necessary to take time to consider what the Bible actually says about the world and the believer's interaction with it and then conform one's life to God's Word rather than man's lists and ideas.

A Biblical Understanding of Worldliness

The Bible *does* give the answer concerning what constitutes worldliness in the eyes of the Lord. Christians today simply need to study, heed, and obey *it* rather than their own traditions and presuppositions.

Consider 1 John 2:15-17. This text is probably the most important text to consider on this topic for two reasons: First, it is the text most often cited by Christians to support their own views concerning worldliness; and second, this text more than any other provides the proper, biblical definition and attitude the Christian should have toward the world.

In these verses, the reader must accurately understand two key words: *love* and *world*. But first, consider the context of this passage. Now that John's readers were consciously aware of their standing in Christ, of their relationship with Jesus, and of their ability to live victorious Christian lives despite Satan's attacks against them (1 Jn. 2:1-14), John warns the believers about the danger of becoming enthralled with and attached to the world system of which they were a part. "Love not the world, neither the things that are in the world," John says.

*The word **love**—*in both instances in verse 15, the word *love* does not entail one's likes or dislikes; rather, it is an act of the will whereby one chooses to exercise benevolence and concern for the wellbeing of someone or something else. It is not used in the sense of "I love Japanese food" or "I love going to football games"—things one cannot help but enjoy. To "love" (*agape*) in this sense is to have a sacrificial care and concern for something. It is a volitional (willful) act of intentional concern for someone or something.

*The word **world**—*the word *world* in this text is translated from the Greek word *kosmos,* which can have a variety of meanings (the earth or universe in general; the human race; the state of human affairs, etc.). What determines its exact meaning is the context. For example, in John 3:16 the "world" refers to *people*, not to the universe, a state of human affairs or a system of philosophy and thought. In 1 John 2:15-17, the context determines that the apostle John is talking about the "system" of things on the earth. Dr. Charles Ryrie put it this way: "that organized system headed by Satan that leaves God out and is a rival to Him." The "world" entails the system of the temporary that finds itself over against the truth as revealed in God and His Word.

So, if one reads this text with a proper understanding of these words in mind and compares this text with others where these terms are used (such as in John 3:16 where we read that "God so *loved* the *world*") and considers the context of 1 John 2:15-17, one will conclude that this text is not talking about the people in the world, nor is it forbidding Christians to enjoy things in life. Rather, to "love not the world, neither the things that are in the world" means a believer must not willfully choose to make those things that are in the world—including those things that are contrary to the person or will of God (those lusts one often strongly desires)—the love, the focus, and the priority of his or her life. Clearly, the intent here is not to separate from everything in the world or to distance oneself from those who are not saved. The meaning of this verse focuses upon where the believer places his love, his concern, his priorities!

In verse fifteen, John describes two things not to love: the *world* and the *things in the world*. What John means by the *world* has already been considered, but what does the apostle mean by the *things in the world*? John himself tells us what he means. He discusses three facets of the "things that are in the world":

Lust of the flesh (desires of the flesh)—"Lust of the flesh" involves the desire for sinful, sensual pleasure that is outside the will of God for any believer. The lust of the flesh is not limited only to sexual desires but to any fleshly appetite for anything that is outside the will of God. To become involved in the lust of the flesh is to satisfy the body at any cost. Paul told Titus that God's grace should lead believers to deny "ungodliness and worldly lusts" (Titus 2:12).

Lust of the eyes (desires of the eyes)—"Lust of the eyes" involves covetousness or the intense desire for material possessions. Notice that this sin primarily manifests itself through *inward* thoughts and desires rather than *outward* actions. To exhibit the lust of the eyes is to covet that which is contrary to the will of God.

The pride of life (pride in possessions or self)—"The pride of life" involves being proud of oneself or one's possessions. This pride is not synonymous with joyfulness in accomplishment but rather with boasting of one's self-worth above one's true worth as found in God's Word. The book of Proverbs characterizes one who exhibits the pride of life as the "fool" or the "froward." "Seest thou a man wise in his own conceit?" Solomon asks. "There is more hope of a fool than of him" (Prov. 26:12). "Conceit" and "the pride of life" are synonymous. The individual full of conceit thinks he is something, when, in God's eyes, he is nothing.

To sum up verse sixteen, the lust of the flesh, the lust of the eyes, and the pride of life involve *anything* that falls outside the will of God or takes one's focus off spiritual things. These three facets of worldliness overtook Eve in the garden of Eden, and even today, thousands of years later, they overtake believers in the church. Yes, John is speaking to believers who *can* (and often do) get caught up in worldliness. The church is not exempt!

So, according to Scripture, the Christian's concern and priorities in life must not lie with the world system or these temporary things in the world. The Bible gives two specific reasons why the believer is to "love not the world":

1. *Love for the world is incompatible with love for God.*

Read the following verses: 1 John 2:15b; Matthew 6:19-21, 24; James 4:4; John 15:18-20. In Matthew 6:19-21, Jesus reveals the importance of laying up "spiritual treasure" in heaven rather than physical treasure while on earth. Why is it so important for believers to strive for spiritual wealth rather than material wealth? Jesus said, "For where your treasure is, there will your heart be also." Just three verses later, Jesus continues, "No man can serve two masters: for either he will hate the one, and love the other; or else he will hold to the one, and despise the other. Ye cannot serve God and mammon [wealth]." The principle here is not difficult to understand. If one is consumed and enthralled with physical happiness or material possessions, he or she has lost sight of the greater importance of spiritual things.

The world system hates God and, therefore, hates those who are followers of Christ. If a believer's life is comfortably conforming to the surrounding world system, then he must step back and discover where his affection actually lies. Jesus told His disciples, "If ye were of the world, the world would love his own: but because ye are not of the world, but I have chosen you out of the world, therefore the world hateth you" (Jn. 15:18-20). James asked the believers in the early church, "Know ye not that the friendship of the world is enmity with God? Whosoever therefore will be a friend of the world is the enemy of God" (Jas. 4:4). To be an enemy of God is certainly a serious matter! Yet the Word of God makes it plain that a believer cannot love the world system and simultaneously strive to effectively attain spiritual goals. Even though a Christian might feel as though he is able to love the world *and* love Jesus Christ at the same time, God's Word declares that this is not possible and the world system is to be rejected by the child of God. "Love not the world" because to love the world is to dishonor Christ. No believer can serve two masters.

2. The world is only temporary.

Consider 1 John 2:17 and 2 Peter 3:10-14. The second reason why the believer is commanded to "love not the world" is because the world in which he lives is only temporary. John told the believers, "And the world passeth away, and the lust thereof" (1 Jn. 2:17). John, an expert in the doctrine of eschatology, not only understood that the world is presently decaying as a result of man's sin in the Garden, but he also realized that one day, a new heaven and new earth would be created by God. Not only is this world temporary in an immediate respect (things decay; people die) but in a future respect as well—Peter reminds believers that they "look for new heavens and a new earth, wherein dwelleth righteousness" (2 Pet. 3:13). How should this affect God's people today? Peter says because this earth is only temporary, Christians should "be diligent that [they] may be found of Him in peace, without spot, and blameless" (2 Pet. 3:14). Clearly, one's present life should reflect one's spiritual priorities. When God's children live with eternity's values in view, their lives on this earth will be remarkably different from the lives of those who have no hope and are uncertain about the future.

In conclusion, it is evident that worldliness, according to God's Word, entails the following three elements: *idolatry*—placing something of this world ahead of God in one's life; making something temporal of a greater priority than that which is spiritual; *covetousness*—desiring that which God has withheld or forbidden; *conformity*—modeling one's thinking or behavior after the world rather than after the Word and will of God.

So biblically speaking, "worldliness" entails having one's focus/priorities (one's heart and mind) set on desiring and embracing the temporary at the expense of the eternal. It is to become enthralled and attached to the mindset of the world and its temporary pleasures rather than having the mind of Christ and seeking spiritual riches (Col. 3:1-2).

The Effect of Worldliness on the Church

How is worldliness affecting the church today? Clearly, it is affecting the church in many ways, but two particular ways stand out:

1. Churches are appealing to the "lusts" of people.

Sadly, many local churches are attempting to gain bodies by giving people, including unbelievers, what they *want* rather than what they *need*. They are appealing to the senses of those who have no spiritual life, and they are hoping to lure people through the doors of the church by conforming to the world system that is so appealing to them. This can be seen in the neighborhood survey concepts of church planting (going door-to-door and asking people what they want and are looking for in a church) and in the evangelism programs of many churches (appealing to the senses of unbelievers by offering them prizes and incentives to attend church or make a profession of faith). The idea is to use the things that interest the world in order to win people to Christ and get them into the church. Although some people may come to a saving knowledge of Christ this way, it can be argued that this philosophy has ultimately produced a biblically-illiterate and even unregenerate "church" today. It can also be argued (from Scripture) that this is *not* a biblical method for church growth and evangelism (the apostle Paul makes this clear in 1 Thessalonians 2:1-12 and 1 Corinthians 2:4).

2. People are too focused on the temporal rather than the eternal.

While the leadership of many churches is guilty of incorporating worldliness into the programs and outreach of the church, the fault does not only lie with them. So many Christians today view God and the church as a marginal part of their lives. They are engulfed in a worldly outlook on life. They are more concerned about their athletic events, their recreation time, or simply their comfort zone than spiritual disciplines. Because of this, personal Bible study, prayer, and church attendance are not a priority at all in their lives. Attendance at church is more a matter of convenience than a priority. They clearly love the world more than God and His will for them. This results in spiritual backsliding and ineffectiveness in ministry. It also results in discouragement and disunity in the church. God has gifted each believer to function as a part of the whole, and when certain members are not exercising their God-given gifts, then the whole church suffers.

Biblical Examples of Worldliness

The Bible provides the reader with examples of those who were guilty of worldliness and also those who chose the alternative path—dedication to God and priority given to a relationship with Him. Consider the following examples:

Lot—Read 2 Peter 2:7-8 and contrast it with the account of Lot in Genesis 19:1-25. It is interesting that the Bible never records any instances of Lot physically engaging in the wicked sins that marked the people of Sodom, but at the same time, it is evident from his actions that he became completely "worldly" in this thought and life. Even though he did not agree with the outward sinfulness so prevalent around him (the text says his soul was "vexed with the filthy conversation of the wicked"), he had no influence or credibility with the people of Sodom. He was comfortable enough to stay in the city and was more interested in maintaining his status in Sodom than his testimony for the Lord.

Demas—Second Timothy 4:10 is a prime example of how one's love for the world can negatively impact the church. Demas had served as a faithful minister and companion of Paul on his missionary journey, but eventually his love for the world rendered Demas ineffective in ministry. He left Paul and chose to align himself with a system ("this present world") that diametrically opposes the person and work of God. Worldliness not only affected Demas, but it also greatly impacted those who loved him, cared for him, and worked with him in ministry.

The church at Laodicea—Revelation 3:15-17 contains Jesus' personal letter to the local church at Laodicea. This church was so worldly-focused and worldly-minded that those who comprised it felt as though they were "just fine" without a close relationship with Jesus Christ. They were self-deceived into thinking that they were "rich" and "increased with goods," clearly a reference to material things. These material things became their comfort and source of security when, in reality, they were "wretched, and miserable, and poor, and blind, and naked" because their priorities did not lie with their Savior.

Abraham—This Old Testament patriarch is a good example of what it means to reject a worldly lifestyle and an attitude of worldliness. Notice Hebrews 11:8-10. Abraham had many "things" (he was an extremely wealthy man), but he was not tied to them. God was his priority in life. Therefore, when the Lord told him to move, he moved. In faith, he took God at His word.

Job—Another example in the Old Testament of one who was not marked by worldliness is Job. Like Abraham, Job was a wealthy man who enjoyed his possessions, his family, and his life, yet God was still his priority even over his relationships and possessions. When all his worldly "things" were taken from him, Job continued to honor God and rely upon Him.

The disciples of Jesus—Some of Jesus' disciples were wealthy while others were poor, yet each disciple (except Judas Iscariot) chose to make his relationship with Jesus Christ the priority in his life, even if that meant losing some of his wealth or status in the world. Peter told Jesus in Matthew 19:27, "Behold, we (the disciples of Jesus) have forsaken all, and followed Thee." This is true discipleship!

The Remedy for Worldliness

God's Word is not only clear in its command to avoid a worldly life, but it is equally clear in its instructions concerning how to avoid this great enemy of the church. In order to avoid worldliness, God's people need to exercise genuine discipleship and change their thinking!

1. Be a true disciple of Jesus Christ.

Is it possible to be considered a true disciple (follower) of Jesus Christ and simultaneously be guilty of worldliness? This is an important question to consider. Worldliness has invaded the church, and yet all believers are called to be disciples of Jesus Christ. The issue here is not salvation, but service and usefulness to God. Consider Luke 14:25-33, for these words of Jesus say a great deal about the issue of worldliness and discipleship.

The church must always remember that God's perspective is different from man's perspective, and for a Christian to truly be called a disciple of Jesus, he must view his life and actions from

God's perspective. Believers today might think they know what it means to be worldly or not, but if their ideas differ from God's, they will get nowhere. It is very possible for true believers to be so caught up with the world that they are not truly disciples as they should be. Self-examination is vitally important here. Consider from the words of Jesus Himself what it really means to be a true disciple of Christ and the role that "worldliness" or "the world" plays in this process of discipleship. According to the Word of God, *a Christian can only be truly called a disciple of Christ if Jesus is his or her priority in life* (Lk. 14:26, 33). This specifically involves priority over three things:

Priority over Family (v. 26a)

The word *hate* in Scripture can be used one of two ways: an active disgust (whether warranted or unwarranted) or in a comparative sense meaning to "love less." Luke 14:26 employs the comparative usage (a parallel text, Matthew 10:37-38, supports this fact). Nothing should stand in the believer's way of doing what he knows to be right—including his family. Sadly, today, professing Christians are even putting "family time" and "family activities" before the things of the Lord—things such as church attendance or personal Bible study. The Bible records *many* instances where family idolatry brought God's displeasure and ruined man's fellowship with the Lord. Christians need to remember that their families, like their possessions, have been entrusted to them by God. They are stewards of their children and even their relationships with their spouses. Yes, the family—as important as it is—actually can be used by Satan to keep men, women, and children from following Jesus Christ. Followers of Jesus need to be extremely careful not to fall prey to family idolatry. Rather, they must pursue the alternative—they must love God above all else and show their love for Him to their family and to all who are around them. Love for God will produce obedience and faithfulness to Him. One cannot claim to be a disciple of Jesus if his family comes before his love of and obedience to his Savior.

Priority over Self (v. 26b)

By nature, every person is prideful and self-centered. Christians are not exempt from this aspect of the old nature. Everybody wants what they want, when they want it, how they want it, where they want it. And, if anything stands in the way—including God, His Word, His church, or His will—woe be to that which stands in the way!

Yet consider the testimony of the apostle Paul in Philippians 3:4-6. Notice all those things he could have boasted in of himself—his lineage, his education, his popularity, his authority. But he came to the point where he surrendered all that "self" in order to be a true disciple of Jesus Christ: "But what things were gain to me, those I counted loss for Christ. Yea doubtless, and I count all things but loss for the excellency of the knowledge of Christ Jesus my Lord" (Phil. 3:7-9). It is only when the believer surrenders his love of himself that he can truly be called a disciple of Jesus Christ.

Priority over Possessions (v. 33)

The word *forsaketh* does not mean Jesus' disciples were required to actively and immediately throw all their possessions into the trash. Those who believed in Jesus still lived their lives in their houses and owned material possessions. The word *forsake* means "to renounce" as in a comparative sense. Followers of Christ need to have a proper priority in life with regard to their "things" as well as their relationships, for "things" can actually keep one from being a true disciple of Jesus Christ. Satan often uses *things* to keep Christians from the *One* who brings true joy, fulfillment, and happiness.

Consider Matthew 19:16-26. Jesus knew the heart of this man and responded to him accordingly. Notice this rich young ruler's mistakes: First, he failed to understand the Person of Christ—that Jesus was God. Second, he failed to understand that eternal life could not be earned by works. Third, he failed to understand that he was a sinner. Finally, he failed to follow Jesus because he loved "things" too much. Believers today cannot claim to be true disciples of Jesus if their "things" are more important than the very One who has blessed them with those "things."

It is fascinating to notice that these very elements that are essential to true discipleship—making God and His Word the priority over family, self, and possessions—are spelled out as "worldliness" in 1 John 2:15-17 (lust of the eyes, lust of the flesh, the pride of life). This is worldliness as defined by God Himself, and this is what keeps Christians from being true disciples of the Lord Jesus Christ.

2. Transform your thinking.

Romans 12:1-2 spells out the remedy for worldliness in its simplest form: Do not be *conformed*, but rather be *transformed*. To be transformed is to be changed from one thing to another. The apostle Paul exhorts all believers to refuse to take the world as their model for life and ministry. Rather, the person, work, and Word of Jesus Christ should be the believer's model for *all* belief and behavior.

How, exactly, can a Christian be transformed? Paul states it clearly: This is accomplished by *thinking differently*. "Be ye transformed by the renewing of your mind," Paul writes. Simply being a Christian in this life is not enough. Rather, Christians need to change the way they think! Believers must be transformed (changed) by new thinking if they are to fulfill God's perfect and acceptable will for their lives. Put on the mind of Jesus Christ (Phil. 2:3-5). Make Him the priority over family, self, and possessions.

Renewed thinking will lead the believer to "put away" the essential elements of what the Bible defines as "worldliness"—

idolatry, covetousness, and conformity to the world system and the things of the world. When a Christian embraces the mind of Christ—a *biblical* worldview rather than a self-centered and humanistic worldview—he or she will refuse to entertain beliefs or engage in behavior that is inconsistent with the person and plan of God. As a believer immerses himself or herself in God's Word and in a personal fellowship with the Savior, he or she will recognize worldliness for what it is and will choose, instead, to believe and behave in a manner that reflects spiritual *life* rather than darkness.

Conclusion

Christians need to understand that the whole concept of worldliness is not a man-made list of "do's and don'ts"; rather, it centers around where one's focus and priorities lie! Are one's priorities set on the temporal—the things of the world—or the eternal—the things pertaining to spiritual life and godliness? A focus on the temporal (the self-centered fulfillment of the flesh) is destroying the church today. It is essential that the believer biblically define and deal with worldliness in order to become a true disciple of Jesus Christ and overcome this great enemy of the church.

Enemy #5: Apathy/Indifference

What Is Apathy or Indifference?

In its simplest form, the word *apathy* entails a lack of concern. When one is apathetic toward something, he or she does not really care or show any involvement or emotion. The word *indifference*, or *indifferent*, is similar in that it entails a lack of interest or concern on the part of a person. It means that one feels that a particular subject is unimportant and non-essential to his or her life. So, when using the terms *apathy* and *indifference* in the realm of Christianity or practical theology, the idea is this: A Christian really does not feel as though the church (or his relationship to God, for that matter) is very important to his life; he is not concerned about his spiritual life and walk with God.

How Is Apathy or Indifference Manifested in the Church Today?

The effect of apathy and indifference on the church in general and on the lives of Christians in particular has been devastating. Consider two primary ways in which this great enemy of the church has manifested itself in the lives of God's people:

1. Biblical Illiteracy

The general lack of biblical literacy in our twenty-first century Western culture is staggering. While professional pollsters have gathered data and reported that a vast ignorance of the Bible and Christianity exists in the United States, one only needs to converse with even other Christians to realize that people have very little knowledge of the Christian faith in general and of the Bible in particular. Sadly, professing Christians are some of the most guilty violators—they seem to know almost nothing about God and His Word except for the clever "one-liner" phrases that permeate so much of Christian conversation. Whether this biblical illiteracy is due to a lack of education in the church or to a lack of personal time in God's Word, the bottom line is this: Many people do not seem to care about learning more of the very faith they profess to believe.

2. General Spiritual Malaise

A lack of concern for spiritual things and a lack of proper priorities in life are the "rotten fruit" of apathy and indifference, and this "rotten fruit" is evident in the lives of professing Christians and in their relationship to the church and to God Himself. In the broader spectrum of the church, one can see apathy and indifference manifested by the lack of good, Bible-teaching churches that exist. At the local church level, one can see apathy and indifference manifested through the attitude of people toward their church and the lack of priority they give it in their lives and the lives of their families. On an individual level, one can see apathy and indifference manifested through the lack of personal time devoted to spiritual disciplines. People do not seem to care about faithful attendance to a good, Bible-believing church, and they care little about spending time in prayer and study of the Scriptures in their personal lives each day.

Biblical Examples of Apathy/Indifference

The Bible records several examples of those who demonstrated an attitude of apathy and indifference in their lives. Whether manifested through an inward heart attitude or through outward actions, this particular enemy of the church is dangerous to the spiritual well-being of God's people.

King Jeroboam's new worship center and worship system (1 Kings 12:25-33)—Jeroboam was afraid that the Israelites who went to Jerusalem to worship the Lord (as they were supposed to do) would return again to Rehoboam, king of Judah. Jeroboam, therefore, established a new worship system with new gods and a new priesthood and informed the Israelites that it was "too much" for them to travel to Jerusalem. Instead, they only needed to travel to Bethel or Dan to worship one of the two calves of gold. First Kings 12:30 is the key here, for although King Jeroboam had ulterior motives for devising and implementing a perverted worship system, clearly the people in general were apathetic and indifferent toward the clear command of God—to worship at Jerusalem. It was much easier for them to "stay put" and not to travel to Jerusalem. They listened to the words of their wicked king.

The Israelites' continual exercise of "religion" apart from any true relationship with God (Amos 4:4-13)—In this text, God tells the Israelites that He is tired of their worthless sacrifices (vv. 4-5). They continued to "go through the motions," and yet their "works" meant nothing to God because their hearts were far from Him. In response, God constantly disciplined them through famine (v. 6), drought (vv. 7-8), pestilence (v. 9), disease and bloodshed (v. 10), etc., yet they would not repent and return to Him. Over and over again God declared, "Yet have ye not returned unto Me, saith the LORD." God's people simply did not care! They were more comfortable living in sin and being chastised by God than changing their hearts and minds.

The parable of the good Samaritan (Luke 10:30-37)—Those who should have known better (the priest and Levite) showed apathy and indifference toward the man who had been beaten, robbed, and left for dead. In other words, the "wise and prudent" (Lk. 10:21) in Israel were totally apathetic and indifferent toward the truth and toward exercising judgment and justice. In contrast, a Samaritan who was despised by the religious establishment of the day exercised an attitude of care and concern for the helpless victim. Jesus used this story to show that those who understand the simple, clear commands of Scripture will do what is right when the opportunity arises and will find themselves commended by God for their attitude and behavior.

The ten lepers cleansed by Jesus (Luke 17:11-19)—In this text, Jesus describes the healing of ten lepers and the gratitude of only one. The one who was grateful—a Samaritan—demonstrated an attitude of thankfulness by returning to Jesus to give thanks and glorify God. He, unlike the others who were healed, was not apathetic or indifferent to the blessing given to him by the Savior. He wanted to *show* His appreciation to Jesus by *taking action* even though it was not convenient for Him—he took the time to return to Jesus and reveal his thankfulness for what He had done for him.

The church at Laodicea (Revelation 3:14-17)—The believers in this local church in Asia Minor were comfortable with themselves and their status and were neither "cold" nor "hot" in their spiritual lives. In other words, they were spiritually apathetic and indifferent, and this showed in their "works" (or lack thereof). They simply did not care what God required of them, for they felt as though they were "rich, and increased with goods, and [had] need of nothing" (v. 17). God's hatred of apathy and indifference is evident in His words: "I would thou wert cold or hot" (v. 15). He adds, "So then because thou art lukewarm, and neither cold nor hot, I will spue thee out of My mouth" (v. 16).

Reasons for Apathy and Indifference in the Church Today

Why is apathy or indifference such a hallmark of professing Christians today? Why do so few believers seem to care about the church and their personal relationship with Jesus Christ? Why do Christians have their priorities so backward? Several reasons exist for this state of the church today.

1. *No Spiritual Life*

Many *professing* Christians are not even truly saved in the first place. When one considers the biblical illiteracy statistics; the lack of faithful, solid, Bible teaching churches throughout this country; the low attendance and lack of priority given to the local church; the anemic interest in doctrine; the miniscule amount of time given to personal Bible study—it becomes obvious that many people who name the name of Christ really have no relationship with Him in the first place.

A true Christian will have a desire to walk with God, to get to know Him better, and to make Him a priority in life. John 10:14, 27 makes it clear that the sheep (Christians) know the Shepherd (Jesus Christ) and follow Him. Notice in this text that the Shepherd is "known of Mine," the sheep "hear My voice," and they "follow Me"—clearly, a relationship built on listening and obeying is the key. This is not to say that sheep never occasionally wander, for they do. However, a life of apathy and indifference reveals no true life in the first place. First John 3:6 explains that the one who is abiding in Christ (enjoying unbroken fellowship with Him) is not sinning; however, the one who habitually sins not only is known by a lack of fellowship with Jesus, but no basis for fellowship has ever been established in the first place—this person has not "seen Him, neither known Him."

Also, a true believer will enjoy and anticipate fellowship with brothers and sisters in Christ. He will want to gather with likeminded Christians where God's Word is taught and God's people come together to "consider one another to provoke unto love and to good works" (Heb. 10:24). The Holy Spirit places a love for brothers and sisters in Christ into the heart of believers, and one who has no desire to encourage, edify, and fellowship with other saints is likely not a believer at all.

2. *A Self-Centered Culture*

While it is true that much of the apathy and indifference so prevalent in the church today result from a lack of any spiritual life in the first place, it is very possible for a Christian to occasionally find himself or herself the victim of this great enemy of the church. Sadly, the proud, individualistic, and self-serving culture in which the believer finds himself often molds him into worshipping the god of *self* rather than the one, true God. Today, society tells people that nobody really matters more than **themselves**, and what one *wants* and what *feels good* are more important than what one knows to be right and truly good. People have been brainwashed by the culture into believing that they alone matter—that as long as a person is happy, all is well. It is no wonder, then, that even believers can become apathetic and indifferent to spiritual things when those things conflict with one's own comfort or interests. What one *feels* (his emotions) takes precedent over what one *knows to be right* (the truth).

3. *No Fellowship with Jesus Christ*

A lack of fellowship with Jesus Christ is the root cause of all true believers' apathy and indifference toward spiritual things. It is not possible for a true Christian to be walking in the Spirit and abiding in fellowship with Jesus Christ while simultaneously having no interest in spiritual things or in doing what is right. The apostle Paul exhorted the believers in Galatia, "Walk in the Spirit, and ye shall not fulfil the lust of the flesh" (Gal. 5:16). He added in verse twenty-five, "If we live in the Spirit, let us also walk in the Spirit." A Christian who is yielded to the Holy Spirit as he is abiding in Jesus Christ will be serious about truth and about honoring Jesus through his thoughts, beliefs, and actions. Conversely, a Christian who is not yielded to the Spirit and abiding in Jesus Christ can easily find himself apathetic and indifferent toward pleasing God and living in a manner consistent with His will.

The Biblical Response to Apathy/Indifference

How is the Christian to battle this heinous enemy of the church? How can he gain the victory over apathy and indifference toward spiritual things? God knows that His children will struggle with this at times, so His Word provides the believer with instruction concerning how to overcome this formidable foe.

1. Wake Up!

Christians must "wake up" and get sober about their spiritual well-being and gain an understanding of what is truly important in life. Notice Romans 13:11-14, for this is a crucial text to understand when considering apathy and indifference in the Christian life. Here, the apostle Paul begins with an assumption—that believers "know the time" in which they live (v. 11). Sadly, many Christians fall too far short of even "knowing the time." The time in which we live is marked by man-centeredness, ignorance of the truth, idolatry, "calling evil good, and good evil," etc. To "know the time" is to be cognizant of the fact that the world system of belief and behavior is not a friend of Jesus Christ or His followers. God calls His children to snap out of their lethargy and wake up to righteous living. This is accomplished by:

"Put on" Jesus Christ (v. 14).

Or, another way to put it is to "put on the armour of light" (v.

12). To "put on Jesus Christ" or to "put on the armor of light" is an act of the will; it is a continual, daily exercise. It is to hear and heed the Word of God through personal study of His Word and to communicate with the Lord through prayer. Spiritual fruit will only become a reality when the believer chooses to abide in Christ (Jn. 15:4-5).

Refuse to make provision for the lusts of the flesh (v. 14).

Or, another way to put it is to "cast off" the works of darkness (v. 12). Notice 1 Corinthians 15:33-34, for in this similar text Paul exhorts the believer to wake up to righteous living and stop sinning. This, too, is an act of the will—it is not automatic. It is a continual, daily act. Why? Because the world, the flesh, and the devil are never taking a break. God's Word describes the Christian's struggle with sin as a battle. It is not easy, but one can have victory with God's help. The key is a *willingness* to follow Jesus and a *yieldedness* to His will, which will lead to "putting on" the proper armor to fight and win (Eph. 6:11ff.) and "putting off" the desires of the natural flesh. When a believer "wakes up" and does these things as he is in fellowship with Jesus, his walk before God and others will be honest and truthful (v. 13).

Wake up! Wake up to spiritual life; wake up from spiritual apathy and lethargy, and wake up to a sense of immediacy and urgency in the Christian life; wake up to righteous living—a life that reflects the Savior. Believers need to stop living in their own dream world and face reality as God defines it. In so doing, they will find true satisfaction as they bring God glory in all their thoughts, attitudes, priorities, and behavior.

2. Get Rid of Idols in the Life.

Again, every Christian must realize that ultimately, the enemy of apathy and indifference stems from idolatry—the idolatry of "self." When "self" gets in the way, then spiritual things will always take a back seat in one's life. The apostle John ended his first letter with these words: "Little children, keep yourselves from idols" (1 Jn. 5:21). Of course, an idol in the life of a Christian is *anything* that takes precedent or priority over God in one's life. Notice that in 1 Thessalonians 1:5-10, the hallmark of these Thessalonian believers was their total *lack* of apathy and indifference. The apostle Paul was thankful for their zeal (v. 3) and their testimony for Christ and their impact on others (vv. 7-8). This all stemmed from their salvation as they turned *from idols* to serve the one, true God (v. 9).

3. Walk with Christ.

Or, in other words, abide in Him. As noted earlier, it is not possible to be apathetic and indifferent toward spiritual things (including the church) while actually abiding in Jesus Christ and walking with Him. When a believer is in fellowship with Christ, he or she will be awake and will not be guilty of idolatry. The result is a genuine interest in spiritual things, and the fruit of the Spirit will be a product of such a life. Notice John 15:4-5. Abiding in Jesus Christ (fellowship with Him) is the only way to bring forth spiritual fruit—the opposite of apathy and indifference. It is interesting to note that Jesus' command to the apathetic church at Laodicea was to "be zealous" and "repent" (Rev. 3:19). He added, "Behold, I stand at the door, and knock: if any man hear My voice, and open the door, I will come in to him, and will sup with him, and he with Me" (Rev. 3:20). The answer to apathy and indifference is renewed fellowship and communion with God. The Lord *wants* fellowship with His own. He is always at the door waiting to commune with those who know and love Him. Yet this fellowship can only be a reality as believers are walking with Him and abiding in Him through study of His Word, prayer to Him, and fellowship with other believers of like faith.

Conclusion

Clearly, apathy and indifference toward spiritual things are serious enemies of the church today. To be apathetic and indifferent means either one does not know Jesus Christ in the first place or one is not walking in fellowship with Him. Christians need to wake up, to get rid of idols in their lives, and to walk with Christ each day. To do this is an act of the will whereby one chooses to do what is right and refuses to allow apathy and indifference to be a hallmark of his or her life.

Enemy #6: Distraction/Diversion

The Reality of Distraction

Ask any Christian in any church what is to be the purpose of the church in the world today, and one will receive as many answers as there are churches! Clearly, one of the greatest enemies of the church today can be summed up in the words *distraction* or *diversion*. Why is distraction or diversion such a problem—such an enemy of the church today? It is because when one is distracted or diverted, it keeps him or her from fulfilling the task needed to be accomplished!

Many professing Christians do not understand what they are to be doing as Christians; therefore, they get caught up focusing on everything *but* what they should be doing! They have become distracted and diverted away from fulfilling the very calling God has given to the church.

Why do Christians meet together on the Lord's Day and at other times throughout the week? What are Christians to do when they leave the confines of the church building and live life at home, at school, or at the office throughout the rest of the week?

One of the greatest problems permeating the church today is a failure to understand its purpose. As a result of this misunderstanding, churches are riddled with Christians who possess a shallow understanding of Scripture and a lack of purpose. This often leads believers to get off track and meander aimlessly through life and even become "tossed to and fro, and carried about with every wind of doctrine" that comes along (Eph. 4:14). Obviously, this cannot be God's will for the lives of His children.

The local church plays a vital role in equipping believers to avoid such aimlessness and instability. Yet in order for Christians to fulfill God's will of glorifying Him and shining as lights and testimonies to the world, the leadership of the local church must clearly understand God's will and His directives for the local church body and then communicate this to God's flock.

Several misconceptions exist as to the purpose of the local church in the world today:

1. Some believe that the purpose of the local church is to meet the perceived needs of those in the community. The contemporary trend in planting new churches is to survey the community and discover what the citizens of the community feel they need. Then, the church leaders pattern the new church after the perceived needs of these unbelievers.

2. Some believe that the purpose of the local church is to "save souls" or to "win people to Christ." The major focus of such a church is to pattern the church service to seek and welcome those who are unsaved. Consequently, the majority of the sermons are evangelistic, and the leaders of the church are continually seeking to find new ways or programs to fill the pews with those who do not know Christ.

3. Some believe that the purpose of the local church is to rally for cultural and political reform or renewal. Leaders in these churches focus the energies of the congregation on changing or "Christianizing" the unregenerate culture by stressing the need to boycott, picket, and vote according to a particular platform. These churches are often "issue-oriented," and most sermons center around the need to "take back" America or renew culture.

4. *Some believe that the purpose of the church is to work for the eradication of poverty and implementation of social justice.* They view the church as a social reformation institution that should focus all its energies on the poor, helpless, and needy. They will often use either Matthew 25:31ff. (when, in reality, this is the judgment of the nations—not the church—following the tribulation and return of Christ to earth) or James 1:26-27 (where James is addressing the outwork of true faith) to "proof text" their belief concerning the purpose of the church. Dr. John Whitcomb has said concerning the focus of the church in this age:

> We will never Christianize the world.... When we become sidetracked, preoccupied with lesser things than the true gospel, the Great Commission suffers a staggering loss. We can't do everything. God never told us to do everything. Jesus never tried to improve the Roman Empire. Neither did the apostle Paul or any of the apostles. Their priority was to do what Jesus told them to do: make disciples, baptize them, and teach them to observe all things whatsoever He taught them.... The main goal ... is to obey the Great Commission of Jesus ("The Greatness of the Kingdom," Christian Workman School of Theology, Lecture 8).

Of course, other churches have even different ideas than the aforementioned concerning the purpose of the local church, but what does God's Word teach concerning the purpose—and thus the focus—of the local church?

Biblical Examples of Distraction and Diversion

This particular enemy of the church is not well represented in the Scriptures. In the early church, those who came to know Jesus Christ as Savior were, for the most part, knowledgeable as to their purpose and faithful to their calling. It seems as though *time* has enhanced this particular enemy of the church today. As time has progressed, Christians have become misled and confused concerning their purpose and calling as Christ's body. They have fallen prey to the voices of religious leaders who have extolled social programs or traditions of men above the clear teaching of Scripture. Yet God's Word does provide a few examples of those who were distracted from their purpose and became diverted away from faithfully fulfilling the will of God for His own.

Demas (2 Timothy 4:10)—Demas had been a companion of the apostle Paul on his missionary journey, but he deserted Paul because he "loved this present world." Clearly, Demas became distracted from the work God had called him to do. Rather than focusing on his goal of glorifying God through faithfulness in ministry, he became caught up in the here-and-now. As a result, God could no longer use him.

The Churches in Asia Minor—The believers in the church at Ephesus (Rev. 2:1-7) apparently became so caught up in "doing" that they became distracted from "being" who they needed to be. God wanted their love and fellowship, but they had "left [their] first love." God commended all their "good works" and their exposure of false teachers and false teaching, yet these good deeds actually diverted their attention from communion with the Savior (comparable to the account of Mary and Martha in Luke 10). Jesus addressed the fact that other churches in Asia Minor were distracted as well. For example, the saints in Pergamos (Rev. 2:12-17) and Thyatira (Rev. 2:18-29) became distracted as they tolerated those in their midst who embraced false doctrine. The Christians in Sardis (Rev. 3:1-6) were "dead" in God's eyes even though they were popular in the eyes of the world. Their popularity distracted them from the godly ministry to which Jesus called them.

The Remedy for Distraction and Diversion

The remedy for this problem that plagues the church today is simple: One must clearly understand the purpose of the church and what is to be its focus in the world today. Obviously, if a believer grasps the purpose, the focus, and the objectives of the church, then any distractions or diversions from such a purpose and focus can be easily recognized and avoided.

Believers—*people*—comprise the church. The church is not a building or a program. The church is *people*. Therefore, the purpose of the church, the body of Christ, is the same purpose as that of every individual believer: to bring glory to God. And, one glorifies God by faithfully obeying His Word.

But on the level of the local church, the question must be asked: What are Christians *to do*? When believers come together as an organized body, and then when they disperse out into the world, what are they to be doing? What is to be their focus? This is an important question because one's answer determines one's actions and focus and priorities in life and ministry.

God's Word is clear—***the purpose of the church is to bring glory to God through the ministry of the Word of God.*** When believers gather together on the Lord's Day and at other times throughout the week, the focus of such gatherings must center around the ministry of discipleship. And, when God's people disperse into the world, they must continue to focus on the work of making disciples. Notice several key texts detailing the purpose and objectives of the church:

Acts 2:42-47—This text contains a picture of life in the early church in Jerusalem. Believers devoted themselves to the apostles' teaching, to fellowship, and to prayer. When they gathered together, they worshipped and praised God through their belief and behavior. This fellowship in the Word led to action—particularly, through their love and selflessness shown toward other believers and their testimony and witness to unbelievers.

Acts 20:27-28—Here, the apostle Paul exhorted the elders of the church at Ephesus to feed God's flock. Paul was about to leave the area, and he reminded them that he had declared to them "all the counsel of God" and told them to do the same after his departure. Clearly, the exposition of God's Word was to be the priority of the elders and the focus of the assembly.

Ephesians 4:11-16—Probably the single-most descriptive text relating to the purpose of the local church, these verses describe the focus of all ministry. God gifted the church with leaders "for" (*pros*—"with a view toward") the equipping of the believers "for" (*eis*—"to" or "into," indicating the point reached) the work of the ministry "for" (*eis*) the edification of the body of Christ. In other words, church leaders must equip disciples to minister to others. The local church is to be a training ground for God's people. It is not to be a social club, a gathering place for social programs, or even a venue to attract the unsaved. It is to be a place where Christians are taught God's Word so they can go into the world and teach others.

1 Peter 5:1-3—The apostle Peter charged the elders of the church to "feed the flock of God." Of course, the food to be distributed is the Word of God, not the ideas or opinions of the pastor or any other person. Pastors and teachers in the church are responsible to feed, guide, and protect the flock. To *feed* entails faithful preaching and teaching of Scripture; to *guide* entails exemplary living and leadership; to *protect* entails awareness of enemies and exposure of the same.

So, it is obvious from these New Testament texts and many others (note the pastoral epistles of First and Second Timothy and Titus) that the purpose of the church is to glorify God, and this is accomplished in the local congregation through the ministry of the Word as God's people are equipped to do the work of the ministry. Jesus' "Great Commission" (Matt. 28:18-20) to "make disciples" through evangelism and training is the way in which the church worships God and brings glory to Him.

Conclusion

It is necessary to understand what God has called His children—His church—to do until He returns. Without a proper understanding of the work of the church in this world, one can expend a great amount of energy in various endeavors that take away from the true focus and ministry of the body of Christ. So, to summarize:

1. **Believers must realize that, ultimately, the purpose of the church is to glorify God.**

One's purpose for existence as an individual is to bring glory to God, and because the church is comprised of individuals, the church body as a whole exists to bring glory to Jesus Christ. "Unto Him (Jesus Christ) be glory in the church" (Eph. 3:21). Paul told the believers in the church at Rome to be likeminded so they could "with one mind and one mouth glorify God" (Rom. 15:6). Clearly, everything accomplished by the saints in a local church foremost should bring glory to God.

2. **Believers must realize that the focus of the local assembly is to equip God's people to do the work of the ministry.**

Paul told the Ephesian saints that God gifts the local church with pastor-teachers who then equip the saints to do the work of the ministry (Eph. 4:11-12). The local church is to be a training ground for believers. And, of course, the food that is to be fed is the Word of God (2 Tim. 4:2; 1 Pet. 5:2). In fact, the very epistles of the New Testament were letters written to local churches, and these letters were (and are) to be studied, taught, and obeyed by the saints.

3. **Believers must realize that the "Great Commission" is a charge to make disciples, not just "get people saved."**

Evangelism is an important part of the Great Commission, but it is only one part (Matt. 28:19-20). God saves, not man. Christians are responsible to be witnesses of the person and work of Jesus Christ, allowing God to work in the hearts and lives of men, women, and children. Yet the responsibility of the church goes beyond evangelism. Discipleship is of paramount importance, and such discipleship takes place within the confines of the local church fellowship (2 Tim. 2:2).

God's Word is clear—the purpose of the local church is to glorify God by equipping the saints to go out into the world and be the church in the world. When God's people realize this fact, they will desire to learn more about God, to abide with Him, and to allow Him to produce the fruit of the Spirit in their lives each day.

Notes:

Notes: